D1744846

VAMPIRES

Brandon Robshaw and Rochelle Scholar

Published in association with The Basic Skills Agency

Hodder & Stoughton

A MEMBER OF THE HODDER HEADLINE GROUP

06589

Acknowledgements

Photos: p. 2 © 20thC. Fox/Everett/REX FEATURES; p. 18 © Corbis

Illustrations: Chris Coady

Cover: Joe McDonald/photo of bat supplied by Corbis; photo of tree supplied by Getty Images/Eyewire

With thanks to Dr Tina Rath.

Orders; please contact Bookpoint Ltd, 130 Milton Park, Abingdon, Oxon OX14 4SB. Telephone (44) 01235 827720, Fax: (44) 01235 400454. Lines are open from 9.00–6.00, Monday to Saturday, with a 24 hour message answering service. You can also order through our website www.hodderheadline.co.uk

British Library Cataloguing in Publication Data
A catalogue record for this title is available from the British Library

ISBN 0 340 87146 6

First published 2003
This edition published 2003
Impression number   10 9 8 7 6 5 4 3 2 1
Year   2007 2006 2005 2004 2003

Typeset by SX Composing DTP, Rayleigh, Essex.
Printed in Great Britain for Hodder & Stoughton Educational, a division of Hodder Headline, 338 Euston Road, London NW1 3BH by Bath Press Ltd, Bath.

Contents

1 Buffy

You may know about Buffy Summers.
You may have watched
Buffy the Vampire Slayer on television.
She was born with the
power to fight vampires.

In 1997, Buffy and her mother
moved house.
They moved to Sunnydale.

Every vampire slayer has a watcher.
Buffy's watcher is called Giles.
Giles tells her that Sunnydale
is on top of a gateway to Hell.
It is called the Hellmouth.

Sarah Michelle Gellar plays the famous vampire slayer.
(Look out – he's behind you!)

When Buffy isn't busy with college life,
she is fighting vampires.
The vampires want to bring
an end to the world.

The job of the slayer is to keep
the world safe from vampires.

Buffy is the latest layer
of the vampire myth.
For hundreds of years,
stories about vampires have been told.

And the stories are always changing.

2 What is a Vampire?

The first thing to say about vampires
is they are not real.
Stories about them
have been popular for centuries.
As stories are passed on,
storytellers put their own spin on them.

Today, we think of a vampire
as tall, dark and pale.
We imagine vampires are men.
They have white fangs.
They have black cloaks.
They live in a castle.
Vampires didn't always look like this, though.

Older stories about vampires tell us
they took many forms.
Some were bald and had tails.

There are stories about vampires
from all over the world.
In Romania, vampires had hooves
like horses.
In China, vampires were covered
in white fur.
In Bulgaria, vampires had
only one nostril.

But all vampire stories
have two things in common.
Vampires are the undead,
And they feed on the blood
of the living.

3 Vampire Powers

In many stories,
vampires have supernatural powers.
They can control the weather.

Vampires do not need to breathe.
They can hide underwater for a long time.

For a few hours,
some vampires can change into the shape
of animals.
Some vampires can even fly.

Vampires may live for hundreds of years.
They might have superhuman strength.

Vampires cannot see themselves in mirrors.
They do not show up in photos.
They cast no shadow.

In some stories,
vampires do not like sunlight.
Sunlight can set a vampire on fire
or turn them to dust.
This is because their bones are so dry.

When the sun comes up,
most vampires go back to their coffins.

4 How to Become a Vampire

Vampires do not want to be dead.
The only way for them to stay 'alive'
is to drink the blood of the living.
They bite the neck of their victim.
They suck out enough blood
to keep them going.

The vampire may turn its victim
into a vampire.
This is done by drinking all the victim's blood.
The vampire then bites its victim once more.
The victim is now a vampire.

There are other ways to become a vampire.
Some stories say that
if you are born
between Christmas Day and 6 January,
you will be a vampire when you die.

If you are born with teeth,
you will be a vampire when you die.
If you are the seventh son
of a seventh son,
or the seventh daughter
of a seventh daughter,
you will be a vampire when you die.

If you eat meat from a sheep
that was killed by a wolf,
you will be a vampire when you die.

When you die,
if a cat, dog or a person jumps
over your coffin . . .
you will be a vampire.

5   Vampire Beginnings

Vampire stories are very old.
They have been told in Europe since
the Middle Ages.

The stories became more popular
in the eighteenth century.
A monk named Dom Augustin Calmet
wrote about strange sightings
in Eastern Europe.
He wrote that men who had died
were seen again in their villages.

The men sucked the blood of their relations.
Their relations fell ill.
Many people died.

The villagers had to find a way to stop
the 'undead' coming back.
They dug the men
out of their graves.
They cut off their heads,
pulled out their hearts and burned them.

Stories spread around villages.
People said dead bodies could be heard
grunting in their graves.
Then they came out of their graves.
The dead had eaten their own hands and feet.

They were hungry for food.
They attacked cattle.
They stuffed themselves with bread and flour.
They were thirsty for blood.
Sometimes they would drink so much blood,
it came out of their ears and nose.

These stories may not have been true,
but they were reported in newspapers.
Suddenly, everyone was interested
in vampires.

These early vampires had faces
as red as fire.
They were stinking, dead bodies.
The vampires were always peasants.

They were not like the modern idea
of a vampire.
They didn't have pale faces.
They didn't have white fangs.
They didn't wear black cloaks.
And they didn't live in castles.

So where does the modern idea
of a vampire come from?

6 A New Kind of Vampire

In 1816, some friends were staying
in a villa in Switzerland.
Two were famous poets,
Shelley and Lord Byron.
Lord Byron was pale and handsome.
He always dressed in black.
He was well-known all over Europe.
He was like a pop star.
There was also Mary Godwin,
Shelley's future wife,
and Byron's friend, Dr Polidori.

The weather was terrible.
There were storms and heavy rain.
They were bored.
Byron said they should all write
a ghost story.
Mary wrote *Frankenstein*.

Polidori wrote the first English vampire story.

It was called *The Vampyre*.

Polidori's vampire was called Lord Ruthven.

He was pale, beautiful and a lord.

In fact, he was a bit like Lord Byron.

Polidori and Byron had not been getting along.

Perhaps this was why Polidori

based the vampire in his story on Byron!

When people read the story,

they forgot about the peasant vampire stories.

They forgot about the red faces

and the stinking bodies.

Now they expected vampires

to be tall, pale and dressed in black.

Bram Stoker, the creator of *Dracula*.

7 Dracula

The most famous vampire of all is Dracula.
Vlad Dracula was a real person.
He was born in the 1400s in Transylvania,
in Romania.
In Romanian, dracul means 'devil' or 'dragon'.
Vlad Dracula was the ruler of Wallachia.
He was a cruel ruler.
He killed his enemies in very cruel ways.
Stories about his cruelty were told
long after his death.
However, he was not realy a vampire.

In 1897, an Irish writer called Bram Stoker
wrote a book about a vampire.
He based his vampire on Dracula.

In Bram Stoker's story,
an Englishman goes to Transylvania.
The man, called Jonathan Harker,
meets Dracula.
He finds out that Dracula is a vampire.
Dracula imprisons him in his castle.

Dracula goes to England.
He finds Jonathan's fiancée, Mina,
and her friend Lucy.
He feeds on their blood.
An old man named Van Helsing
tries to save them,
but Lucy dies.

Jonathan escapes from the castle
and returns to England.
He and Van Helsing manage to save Mina.
They nearly catch and kill Dracula,
but he escapes back to Transylvania.

Jonathan and Van Helsing follow
Dracula back to Transylvania.
They find him asleep in his coffin.
They stab him in the heart,
and cut his throat with a knife.
Dracula crumbles into dust.

The book was first made into a film in 1922.
The actor Max Schreck played Dracula.
In the film, he had a bald head,
pointed ears and long fingers.

But the most famous vampire film
was made a few years later.
The actor Christopher Lee played Dracula.
He was very tall – nearly two metres.
His hair was dark and his face was pale.
He wore a black cloak and had white fangs.
This became most people's idea
of what a vampire should look like.

The film was a great success.
It started a new trend in vampire films.
Of all vampire films ever made,
ninety per cent were made
after Christopher Lee's *Dracula*.

8 Corpse to Vampire

In folklore, there are many ways
to stop a corpse becoming a vampire.

Vampires do not like garlic.
Some say that this is because
the white cloves are like white fangs.
Put garlic cloves in a corpse's mouth.
This will stop a corpse
from becoming a vampire.

Coins should be put over a corpse's eyelids.
This will help the body pay for entry
into the world of the dead.
Then they will not try to get back
to the world of the living.

You should turn the body
face down in the coffin.
If the corpse wants to get out,
it will just dig deeper down.

The coffin must be buried
two metres underground.
This makes it harder for a corpse
to climb out.

But what if it does?
How do you get rid of a vampire?

9 How to Get Rid of a Vampire

Buffy the Vampire Slayer is super-strong.
She has amazing fighting skills.

If you are not a vampire slayer,
there are other ways to get rid of them.

You could drive a stake once
through the vampire's heart.
But only once.
If the vampire is stabbed twice,
it will come back to life.

If this does not work,
you could try cutting off its head.
The head and the body must be buried again
in the same grave.

Vampires catch fire quickly
because their bones are so dry.
Crosses and Stars of David
can also burn vampires.

You could also try
sprinkling mustard seeds
on a vampire's grave.
When the vampire comes out,
it will have to count every single seed.
This could take all night!

You could try eating earth
from the vampire's grave.
Rub yourself with vampire blood, perhaps.
Make a cake with vampire blood
and flour.

These are just folk-tales, of course.
Vampires are not real.

Why do people like vampire stories so much?
Perhaps it is because vampire stories
are about our deepest fears.

We are scared of the dark.
We are scared of blood.
We are scared of death.
We are scared of the unknown.

Vampire stories have changed
over the centuries.
What will the twenty-first – century vampire
be like?